A Tale of Two Cities

by CHARLES DICKENS

Abridged and adapted by ANDREA M. CLARE

Illustrated by DICK COLE

 A PACEMAKER CLASSIC

FEARON PITMAN PUBLISHERS, INC.
Belmont, California

PACEMAKER CLASSICS

Robinson Crusoe
The Moonstone
The Jungle Book
The Last of the Mohicans
Treasure Island
Two Years Before the Mast
20,000 Leagues Under the Sea
A Tale of Two Cities

Library of Congress Catalog Card Number: 73-80400

ISBN-0-8224-9228-8

Printed in the United States of America.

Contents

1 The Dover Mail

It was the best of times. It was the worst of times. It was a time when people were beginning to hope. It was a time when people had no hope at all.

George III was the King of England. Louis XVI was the King of France, and Marie Antoinette was Queen. In both countries, the nobility owned the land while poor people worked it. The nobility had money while their workers did not. Kings ate large dinners while poor people starved. This had been going on for so many years that it seemed things would never change.

The year was 1775. The Continental Congress was meeting in America. Europeans heard many stories coming from the Continental Congress. They heard that Americans did not want to pay taxes to the King of England. They heard that these Americans wanted to make their own laws. They heard that the Americans wanted to have a voice in their own government. But America was far away, and the nobility did not listen.

But the nobility should have listened. The sound of the American Revolution was soon to echo around the world. It was to change their very lives.

But the nobility closed their ears to the warning sounds across the sea. In France, the nobility went on taking taxes and food from the people and giving nothing back to them. The King did not care that his people starved. People who had done nothing bad were put to death. Others had their hands or ears cut off. Poor people had no rights at all.

In England, King George III did not take much better care of his people. Many of the people were very poor. They had to rob to live. Killing took place in the streets every night. People were afraid to go out alone.

But one dark night, Mr. Jarvis Lorry had to go out on the roads. Tellson's Bank, where he worked, was sending him from London to Paris. To get across the English Channel, Mr. Lorry had to take a boat from Dover. He got a ride to Dover on the mail coach.

Two other men were in the coach that night. Each man sat as far from the others as he could. No one said anything. All three hid their faces under their hats. In those days, people did not want to be seen by those they did not know. They were afraid of being killed or robbed.

The night was very dark because of a heavy rain. Mud covered the roads and slowed the coach down. Ten miles outside of London, the rain began to let up. A while later, it stopped. The horses were tired as they pulled the coach up Shooter's Hill.

"Get on with you, horses! One more pull and we are at the top," said the man driving the coach. "What time is it, guard?"

"It is ten minutes after 11:00," the guard answered. "Wait! Do you hear a horse coming up behind us?"

The first man stopped the horses. "Yes, I do!" he answered.

The guard readied his gun and waited. The men inside the coach were afraid. Every man listened as the horse came near.

"Stop!" the guard called out. "Stop or I shall fire!"

The horse stopped where it was. A man's voice called out, "Is that the Dover mail? I want to talk to one of the men in the coach. Is Mr. Jarvis Lorry with you?"

Mr. Lorry seemed surprised. The guard walked over to the coach window and gave Mr. Lorry a careful look. "Are you Mr. Lorry?"

"Yes, who wants me?"

"This is Jerry Cruncher, Mr. Lorry. I have a note for you from Tellson's Bank."

Mr. Lorry looked at the guard. "I know this man. Let him come close to us."

The guard called out to Jerry Cruncher. "You may come a step or two this way," he said. "But if you have a gun, don't put your hand near it. Now, come where we can see you."

Jerry Cruncher moved close to the men. He looked at the guard and handed a letter to Mr. Lorry.

"It is all right," Mr. Lorry said to the guard. "I work for Tellson's Bank. May I step out into the light and read this?"

"If you are quick at it!" was the answer.

Mr. Lorry stepped to the ground. He turned to the light and read the letter out loud. " 'Wait for the lady in Dover.' "

"They want me to take your answer back to them," Cruncher said.

"My answer is, 'Brought back to the living.' "

"Now *that* is a funny answer," said Jerry Cruncher, not knowing what to make of it.

"Just take my answer back. They will know it came from me. Be careful now. Good night!"

Mr. Lorry got back into the coach. The other men, afraid that Mr. Lorry was going to rob them, made believe they were asleep. While Mr. Lorry had been talking to Jerry Cruncher, the men hid their money from him.

The coach headed for Dover again. Before long, the guard put his gun away. " 'Brought back to the living!' That is a funny answer all right!"

Mr. Lorry soon fell asleep. When he woke up, it was morning and the coach was pulling into Dover. When he got off the coach, Mr. Lorry went to the Royal George Hotel. He got himself a room, and he asked for another room for a lady. Then, he went to his room, washed up, and shined his shoes. He put on a clean brown suit and went to lunch.

Just as he finished, one of the servants came to him. "A Miss Manette is here. She said she would be happy to see you when you are ready."

Mr. Lorry followed the man to Miss Manette's room. He knocked at the door. A beautiful girl answered it. She was no more than 17 years old. Her long gold hair fell down her back. Her blue eyes were shining. "Please come in, Mr. Lorry," she said. "Do sit down."

"Thank you, Miss Manette," he answered.

"Mr. Lorry, I got a letter from Tellson's Bank. It said that you have learned something new about my poor father. Oh, how I wish I had seen him even once before his death!"

Mr. Lorry moved in his chair. "Yes, child, I know you never saw your father."

"The letter said that I must go to Paris and meet you there. Since I have no family, I asked if I could go with you. I am afraid to go alone."

"I would be happy to watch over you."

"The men at Tellson's Bank said you would tell me what I need to know. They said it would surprise me. But I am ready to hear any news you have for me."

"Your father's story is a hard one to tell. He was a kind Frenchman, a doctor. I knew him for many years. He married a beautiful English woman."

"My mother!" said Miss Manette. "But I lost her when I was only two years old."

"Yes, child, that was your mother. After her death, I brought you to England where friends cared for you. Your mother left this world never knowing what happened to your father. He was called away to help a man one day and never came home."

"But as a child I was always told of his death."

"Your mother wanted to keep you from suffering the way she did. She thought it would hurt you to wonder if your father was living. She never stopped looking for him. She herself was afraid that he might be in the Bastille."

"In the Bastille? Had he done something bad?"

"No, child, in France men may be put in the Bastille because the nobility wants them there. The rest of this story is very hard to tell. Can you bear to hear it?"

"Yes, please go on!"

"We think . . . we think we have found your father. He is living in Paris."

"Oh," cried Miss Manette. "How can this be?"

"I know this is hard for you. I must go to Paris to see for sure if it is your father. He does not look the same. He does not even know his own name. We are asking you to go to Paris to help him. You are all he has."

"I am afraid!" the girl cried. "It will be like bringing my father back from the grave!"

"There, there, my child, you must be strong. Your father needs your help. He is not the same man that he was. He has been in the Bastille for almost 18 years. He was caged in 105 North Tower all that time. That will change any man."

"Where is he now?"

"He is staying with a friend in Paris, a Monsieur Defarge. Your father lives in a small room above a wine shop. No one knows his name. Tomorrow morning we will go to France. We will see him and bring him home with us. You will need to be strong."

"I will try to be strong for him," the girl answered. "Until morning, then, Mr. Lorry. Good afternoon."

"Good afternoon, Miss Manette."

2 The Wine Shop

Monsieur Defarge was standing in front of his wine shop. A wagon, filled with red wine, stopped near him.

"Good day, Monsieur Defarge," said the wagon driver. "I have some more wine for you. I will take it inside the shop."

"Watch out!" Monsieur Defarge called out. "It is going to fall!" But his warning came too late. Some of the wine fell out of the wagon. It hit the ground and splashed all over the street. Red wine covered everything. Some of it rested in little red ponds. The rest of it ran in little rivers between the stones.

All of the people near the shop saw what happened. They stopped working and ran into the street. "Get it before it gets away!" cried one woman. She cupped her hands to catch a little river of wine.

"I can get more this way!" laughed a man. He had his mouth to the ground. The people ran about the street, catching every drop of the red wine that they could.

"Look at me!" cried out a man named Gaspard. He was writing on a wall with the red wine.

"B-L-O-O-D! Don't you think this looks like blood?" Gaspard said.

Many people laughed at Gaspard's joke, but not Monsieur Defarge. The people played their wine-hunting game until the street was dry. When the game was over, their faces, hands, and feet were painted with red wine. The street, too, was red. It would take many weeks for the rain to wash the red off the stones. But these same faces and streets would be covered with red again. The next time, they would be covered with blood. Rain would never wash that away.

Monsieur Defarge crossed the street. He went up to Gaspard and said, "Gaspard, what did you write?"

Gaspard, still laughing, pointed to the word "blood." Monsieur Defarge picked up some mud and covered the word with it. "Call wine, wine," he said. "Do not think that it is blood. The time will come when you will see enough of that." Then, Monsieur Defarge crossed the street again and went into his wine shop.

Madam Defarge was sitting there, knitting. A man in a brown suit was sitting with a pretty woman in the corner. Three men were sitting at a table drinking.

Monsieur Defarge stopped near the three men. "Hello, Jacques," he said.

"Hello, Jacques," the three men answered together.

Monsieur Defarge walked over to the man and woman in the corner. "I will go outside," he said in a quiet voice. "Follow a few steps behind me."

Monsieur Defarge went out the back door and stepped into a small yard. The yard was closed in on all sides by old houses. The wine shop was housed on the bottom floor of one of these buildings. And Doctor Manette was on the top floor. To get to him, they had to use another outside door. Monsieur Defarge waited there for Mr. Lorry and Miss Manette. When they were all together, Monsieur Defarge said, "He is on the top floor. It is hard to climb up these steps. Be careful."

They talked in quiet voices as they walked up to the first landing. "Has he changed very much?" Mr. Lorry asked.

"Changed!" cried Monsieur Defarge. "You may not even know him!"

"Is he alone?"

"Yes, he is alone. He has been alone for so many years that he is afraid of people."

They climbed up the dark steps until they came to the top floor. Monsieur Defarge went to the door and knocked. "I want to make as much noise as I can before we go in. He will be afraid if we surprise him."

As Monsieur Defarge opened the door, Miss Manette pulled away from Mr. Lorry. She stepped back from the door and would not go in. "I am afraid. Please, I don't want to go in."

"Be strong, child. Your father needs you," said Mr. Lorry, taking her hand. He pulled her into Doctor Manette's room. Monsieur Defarge closed the door behind them.

The room was very dark. The only light came in through a small door in the roof. At first, Mr. Lorry and Miss Manette could not see the doctor. But then their eyes got used to the dark. Across the room, the old man was sitting at a small table. He was tapping a nail with an old hammer. The white-haired old man was busy making shoes.

Monsieur Defarge walked over to the doctor and stood near him. Doctor Manette did not know he was there. At last, Monsieur Defarge said, "Good day!"

The old man looked up at Monsieur Defarge. "Good day," he answered in a far-away voice. The doctor looked back at his work. He kept tapping the small nail.

"I want to let more light in here," said Monsieur Defarge. "Can you stand it?"

"If you let it in, I *must* stand it."

Monsieur Defarge opened the little door in the roof. An arrow of sunshine fell into the room, lighting up the doctor's head and his table. The old man put up his hand to keep the light out of his eyes. Miss Manette could see her father better now. He was very thin. His eyes had a lost look about them. But they were blue like her own. The doctor looked down at his table again and began tapping. Mr. Lorry went over to him.

"A friend has come to see you," said Monsieur Defarge. "Show Mr. Lorry the shoe you are making."

Mr. Lorry took the shoe in his hand.

In a soft voice, Mr. Lorry asked, "Did you always to make shoes?"

After a few minutes the doctor answered. "No. I just learned. I asked the guards if I could learn. It gave me something to do." The old man took the shoe back from Mr. Lorry.

"Doctor Manette, do you know who I am?"

At the sound of his own name, the doctor dropped the shoe on the floor. He sat there for a long time, looking at Mr. Lorry. He seemed to know him one minute and not know him the next. The poor man was not sure of anything.

While the doctor sat looking at Mr. Lorry, Miss Manette moved near the little table. She stood beside her father and watched him. Afraid to look at him at first, she now looked at him with love. But the old man did not even know she was there.

At last, the doctor started back to work. He picked up the shoe from the floor. Then he turned to pick up his hammer. As he turned, he saw a woman's dress. His eyes moved up the dress until he saw the girl's beautiful face. At first, the doctor was afraid. Then he seemed surprised. "Who are you?" he asked.

The beautiful girl kissed him and sat on the floor at his feet. She placed her hand on his arm. He pulled his arm away from her and looked at her yellow hair. Little by little, the old man moved his hand near her. Then he petted her hair.

But all at once the old man began shaking his head. "No, no," he said, "it is not her. It cannot be her." He put his hand to his neck and took off an old black string. A small piece of paper was tied to it. He opened the paper and took out two long gold hairs. Then he took Miss Manette's hair into his hand. "This hair is gold, too. It is the same. But how can it be like hers? Was it you? No, you are not old enough. Her hair would be white by now—white like my own."

The doctor took a careful look at the girl. He turned her face so that the light would shine on it. The doctor talked in a quiet voice. "She rested her head on my arm the night I was called away. When they brought me to the North Tower, I found these hairs on my coat. I kept them and hid them. I wanted to keep them as a present from her. What is your name, my child?"

"I will tell you soon, but not now. I will tell you who my mother was and who my father is. I think I may look like a woman you once loved. Thank God for it!"

Miss Manette put her arms around her father's neck and kissed him. The girl and her father began to cry in each other's arms.

At last, she looked up at Mr. Lorry. "Please get a coach ready for us. It is time to go back to England. You were so kind to bring me here."

Soon the coach was ready. The men helped Doctor Manette down the steps and into the yard. Miss Manette carried his hammer, nails, and shoes. They went through the wine shop and out to the street. Madame Defarge, still knitting, watched the old man and the girl get into the coach.

"Good day, Monsieur Defarge," said Mr. Lorry as they pulled away from the wine shop. "Thank you for all your help."

The coach moved on through Paris. Mr. Lorry looked at the old man sitting beside him—a man saved from death. *Are you happy that you are brought back to the living?* he thought. And in his own head he thought he heard the old man answer, *I don't know.*

3 Five Years Later

The courtroom in London was buzzing with voices. The room was so full that Mr. Sydney Carton had a hard time getting through the door. He pushed his way through red-eyed men, old ladies, and small children. Mr. Carton watched their faces as he went by them. And he listened to what the people were saying.

"Charles Darnay is coming up next," one man said. "He will be tried for being a spy—a spy for the French."

"We will have fun watching him killed tomorrow," the man sitting next to him said. "Darnay will be pulled through the streets of London by horses. That will break his arms and legs. Then he will be hanged."

"Is that all?" the first man asked, with a wild look in his eyes.

"No, while he is still living, they will take him down. Then Darnay will watch as they cut his insides out. But it will not hurt him too long, because then they will cut his head off!"

The man clapped his hands together and laughed. "Oh, it will be so much fun. I have not seen a killing like this since last Christmas!"

Mr. Carton looked at the men. "*If* the jury finds Mr. Darnay guilty," he said.

"Oh," was the answer. "They will find him guilty. Don't be afraid of that!"

Sydney Carton pushed on to the front of the courtroom. He took his place beside Mr. Stryver, the defender. "These people want to see a killing," Sydney Carton said. "Do you think you can prove that Darnay is not guilty?"

"I don't know," answered Mr. Stryver. "The prosecutor has witnesses to prove that the prisoner is guilty. But their stories don't prove anything. I don't believe a one of them! If only I can show that to the jury."

Just then, the judge came into the courtroom. The buzzing voices stopped. A minute later, a door opened in the front of the courtroom. Two guards came in with the prisoner.

The people in the courtroom had been waiting all day to see the "spy." As Charles Darnay came into the room, their hungry eyes followed him. People near the front of the room stood up to get a better look at him. People near the back climbed on chairs. Fathers held their children up so they could see. Once in a while, a voice cried out, "Guilty! Guilty! Cut off his head!"

Mr. Carton looked at the prisoner. Charles Darnay did not seem to be afraid. He was standing still, looking at the faces of the people. If he heard their cries, he did not show it.

The prisoner was a good-looking man, about 25 years old. His long brown hair was tied at the back of his neck. *He looks very much like me,* thought Sydney Carton. Carton tapped Mr. Stryver and said, "He looks a lot like me. Don't you think so?"

Mr. Stryver looked from Sydney Carton to Charles Darnay. "Well, what do you know! You do look very much like each other. Yes, you two could be brothers."

"Let us have quiet in the courtroom!" called out the judge. "Mr. Charles Darnay says he is not guilty of spying for the King of France. He says he did not tell the French about guns being sent to North America. Now, let us begin this hearing. The prosecutor may start."

"My friends of the jury, I call my first witness," said the prosecutor. "Will Mr. John Barsad come to the stand." Mr. Barsad was sitting in the front row beside the other witnesses. His face was cold and hard.

"Mr. Barsad, do you know the prisoner?" the prosecutor asked.

"We have been friends for five years."

"Please tell the jury about the letters you found."

"Well," Mr. Barsad began, "a servant of Mr. Darnay brought them to me. He said he found the letters in Mr. Darnay's suit pocket. The letters told how many guns England was sending to America. Mr. Darnay was planning to take the letters to France. He is a spy! He is a spy for France!"

The voices in the room echoed Mr. Barsad's words, "Spy! Spy!"

"Quiet!" cried the judge. "Do you have anything to ask the witness, Mr. Stryver?"

"Yes," he answered as he walked up to John Barsad. "Tell me, Mr. Barsad, have you ever been a spy?"

"No!"

"Have you ever been a prisoner?"

"Yes."

"What for?"

"Because I had no money. I could not pay my bills."

"How many times were you a prisoner?" Mr. Stryver asked.

"Five or six times," Barsad answered.

"Did Mr. Darnay ever give you any money?"

"Yes."

"Did you ever pay him back?"

"No."

"Are you sure you did not plant the letters in his pocket? If Mr. Darnay was out of the way, you would not have to pay him back. Is that not so?"

"I would never do anything like that!" Barsad roared, his face growing red.

"That is all, Mr. Barsad. Thank you."

The prosecutor called Miss Lucie Manette next. Miss Manette had been sitting in the courtroom with her father. When her name was called, she stood up. Doctor Manette stood with her, holding her hand. The doctor looked strong.

"Miss Manette, look at the prisoner," said the prosecutor. "Do you know him?"

The beautiful woman turned to Mr. Darnay. She gave him a soft look. "Yes, I know Mr. Darnay. He was on the boat from Calais to Dover. I was taking my father back to England. When this good man came on board, he saw my father. The doctor was very sick then. I was trying to keep the wind off of him. The prisoner was kind enough to help me. I hope what I say will not hurt him. He was so good to me!" Her eyes filled with tears.

"Please tell us what the prisoner said to you that night."

"He told me that he had to go between England and France often. He did not tell me about his work. He said that other people might be hurt if he talked about it."

"And did he say anything about America?" the prosecutor asked.

It was hard for Miss Manette to go on. She was afraid that her words would make the jury find him guilty. "Yes, he told me how the American Revolution started. He believed that the American people were right. But he did not hurt anyone."

"That is all, Miss Manette. Thank you."

The prosecutor called his last witness. A short, heavy man took the stand. He said, "One night in November of 1775, I was in a tavern near Dover. Darnay was sitting in one corner. Later that night, two men came in and sat with him. I heard them talking. They said that guns were on their way to America!"

The people in the courtroom jumped up and pointed to Charles Darnay. *"Guilty! Guilty! Hang him!"* they cried.

"Are you sure that the person you saw that night was Charles Darnay?" said the prosecutor.

"Yes, quite sure."

"Do you want to ask the witness anything, Mr. Stryver?" asked the judge.

"Yes," Mr. Stryver answered. "Are you quite sure it was the prisoner you saw that night?"

"Quite sure. I have never seen anyone else who looks like him. I am very sure he was the man!"

"Then I must ask you to look at my friend, Sydney Carton."

Mr. Carton stood up, and all the faces in the courtroom turned to him. Words of surprise echoed around the room.

"Well, do you think Mr. Carton looks like Mr. Darnay?" Mr. Stryver asked.

"Yes, very much. I find it hard to believe!"
"Shall we then try Mr. Carton as a spy, too?"
"I ... I don't know," the witness answered.

"You must have been drinking in the tavern that night. Can you say for sure that you saw Mr. Darnay and not Mr. Carton?"

"I don't know what to say . . . . I think . . . . I *thought* . . . . I don't think I can say for sure."

"Thank you," said Mr. Stryver, smiling. "You may step down."

It was now up to the jury. The jury left the courtroom to talk about what they had heard. After a long time, they came back in. The people in the courtroom stopped talking so they could hear every word. They were sure the jury would find Darnay guilty. Happy faces watched the jury, knowing that tomorrow they would watch a killing. Miss Manette gave the prisoner a loving look. The thought of his death made her feel sick inside.

Then the judge turned to the jury and asked, "How do you find the prisoner?"

"We find him not guilty!"

The people in the courtroom jumped up. Surprise showed on their faces. There would be no killing tomorrow. There would be no blood. The people would have to wait for that. They hurried from the courtroom. As they buzzed away, they looked like hungry flies hunting for their dinner.

When the people were gone, Mr. Lorry and the Manettes went up to Mr. Darnay. "We are very happy for you," said Mr. Lorry.

"Thank you," Mr. Darnay answered. "And thank you, Mr. Stryver. You have saved me." Mr. Darnay walked to the street with his new friends. He helped Miss Manette and her father get into a coach.

After they left, Charles Darnay stood alone, wondering where to go. Then Mr. Carton came out of the courtroom and saw him. "You must be hungry, Mr. Darnay," he said. "Let me show you a tavern that has very good food."

Sydney Carton took Charles Darnay's arm. Soon they were in a small tavern eating dinner and drinking wine.

"We look so much the same," said Carton, filling his cup with wine.

"Yes, and that helped me today," answered Darnay. "I was afraid they were going to find me guilty. I am very happy to be here this evening."

Carton tried to smile. But a smile would not come to his face. He was a man who had not smiled in a long time. "You are happy, Mr. Darnay," he said. "That is good. I would like to be happy, too. But I have nothing to be happy about, nothing in the world. Nothing, that is, but wine."

Carton picked up his cup and took a long drink. "When I drink enough of this, I may be happy, too."

Darnay did not know what to say. "But Mr. Carton . . . . There is more to life than wine. What about your loved ones? What about those who care for you?"

"No one cares for me, Mr. Darnay. And I have no one to care for. I care only for my wine."

Carton finished his wine and filled his cup again. "I am not like you, Mr. Darnay. I wish I were. But I am not. You have a lady who cares for you. And what a lady! Miss Manette had such a look of suffering in her eyes today. Oh, to be looked at by that loving face! How does it feel to have a beautiful woman smile at you? I would go to my death for such a woman! How happy I would be knowing she had kind thoughts about me."

Darnay looked at Carton straight in the eye. "A man must like himself before others can like him."

"It is too late for me now," said Sydney Carton. "There is nothing good left in me. I am a lost man."

The two men were quiet for a minute. Then Darnay stood up. "I must go now, Mr. Carton," Darnay said. "It is getting late. But I do want to say one thing to you. Don't give up hope. If you believe in what you can do, others will believe in you, too. Good night, Mr. Carton."

Charles Darnay got up from the table and took care of his bill. As he left the tavern, he heard Sydney Carton call for more wine.

4 The Marquis St. Evremonde

Gaspard was taking water from a well near the wine shop in Paris. His small boy was playing near him. All at once, Gaspard heard cries coming from the people down the road. "Watch out! The Marquis is coming this way!"

Gaspard looked up to see a coach hurrying into town. " It is always the same," he said. "The Marquis always comes too fast. We don't even have time to get out of his way. One day he is going to kill one of us!"

Gaspard called to his boy. "Quick! Get out of the road!"

The Marquis was coming home from a meeting with other nobility in Paris. He went every Saturday afternoon, even though he did not like the parties. He had to go because he was part of the nobility. So every Saturday, the Marquis suffered through the party, then hurried back to his country home.

This afternoon, the Marquis looked from his coach as it went down this little street. "Hurry up!" he cried to his driver, smiling. "I love to watch these people run! Drive close to them! See how afraid they are!"

A few feet in front of the coach, the Marquis saw a father with his boy. The two were running as fast as they could. All at once, the coach hit something. The people in the street let out a loud roar. The horses kicked and jumped.

"What is the matter now?" asked the Marquis, sticking his head out of the window. He watched as Gaspard picked up a child from under the horses' feet. Gaspard laid the child near the well and began to cry.

"Marquis, we have killed the child," said the driver.

"And why is that man crying?" the Marquis asked with a cold voice. "Is it his child?"

Gaspard jumped up from the ground and came running at the Marquis. "You killed him!" he cried. "You killed my boy!"

The Marquis took out some gold pieces. "You people don't take very good care of your children. That is all I can say. You are always in the way. Here, take this!" The Marquis threw the gold at Gaspard. "Now get out of the way of my coach, you dogs!" he roared at the people. "Driver, go on!"

The coach hurried on its way. Gaspard stood in the street, crying. Monsieur Defarge walked over to him. Madame Defarge, still knitting, watched them both.

The Marquis hurried through the city and into the country. The road to his chateau was long. The sun set before the coach pulled up in front of the Marquis' home. As it stopped, a servant opened the front door of the chateau.

"Has Charles come in from England?" the Marquis asked. "He planned to be here by now."

"He will be here soon," the servant answered.

A few minutes later, the Marquis sat down alone to a large dinner. He was finishing the first part of his supper when he heard a noise outside. His nephew, Charles Darnay Evremonde, stepped from a coach and came into the chateau. Soon, the two men were sitting at the dinner table together.

"I find it hard to face the people around us here," Darnay said. "They all seem so afraid of us."

"That shows you how great our family is. We Evremondes keep those people trained, just like dogs! We keep them in their place. Like dogs. *Just like the dogs they are!*"

"But, Uncle," said Darnay, "this is not right. We are hurting the people around us. We hurt anyone who gets in the way of our own fun. We should not be like this. We should help these poor people. We can end their suffering. And we can keep them from starving."

"You say we are hurting them?" asked the Marquis with a cold smile.

"Yes, we were hurting them even when my father was still living. I feel tied to a government that I am afraid of. I want to stop what it is doing, but I can't. I want to follow my mother's last wish and be kind to these people. I need help to make things right for them."

"You will never get help from me," said the Marquis. "You are my nephew. And you are part of the Evremonde family. But if you wish to help these people, then I must look upon you as one of them. I will give you no help!"

"Then I give up all that ties me to France. I want no part of the family's money or name. From now on I will be Charles Darnay, not Charles Evremonde."

"And how do you plan to live in England?" said the Marquis.

"I will work—something that you and the nobility here do not know."

"Yes, many Frenchmen like it in England," said the Marquis. "Do you know a Doctor Manette in London?"

"Yes," Darnay answered, surprised.

"Yes," echoed the Marquis, smiling. "Servant, show my nephew to his room!"

The Marquis got up from the table. "Yes, you know a doctor and a beautiful girl. So your new hopes begin. Good night!" The Marquis went to his bedroom, laughing.

The night was very warm. The Marquis stood near his open bedroom window and let the wind blow across his face. At last, he went to bed.

In the morning, Charles waited for his uncle at the breakfast table. When the Marquis did not come, the servants went to wake him. They found him in bed, with a knife through his heart. Next to him was a note: "Death to the Marquis—Jacques."

5 Secret Words of Love

A year went by. Charles Darnay was doing very well as a French teacher in Cambridge. He had gone back to England the day his uncle, the Marquis, was killed.

Darnay visited the Manettes often. He saw a great change in Doctor Manette. The old man was now very strong. The light had come back to his eyes. Lucie had helped her father get better with all of her loving care.

But even after living in England for six years, the doctor never talked about France. He became sick if anyone talked about prisoners. When the doctor thought about the Bastille, he would close himself in his room. Lucie would then hear her father tapping with his hammer again. There was nothing she could do to bring him out of his shell. Only time could end his suffering.

Darnay was in love with Lucie. He had been ever since he saw her in the courtroom a year before. But even with his visits, he never told Lucie of his love. This summer day, Darnay rode from Cambridge to London to talk with Doctor Manette. Darnay knew that Lucie would not be home until later that afternoon.

"Charles, how happy I am to see you," said the doctor as he opened the door. "We were hoping you would be in town soon."

"How good you look, Doctor Manette," Darnay answered.

"Lucie is not home right now, but please come in and sit down." Darnay followed the doctor into the living room and sat down near the window.

"Doctor, I knew Miss Manette would not be home. I wanted to talk with you alone."

"Yes?" said the doctor, surprised.

"Doctor Manette, I love Lucie very much. I would do anything for her."

"Have you told Lucie how you feel?"

"No," Darnay answered. "I know that Lucie loves you with all her heart. In you, she loves both her mother and her father. I know that you feel the same strong love for her. I don't want my love to come between you."

"Thank you," answered the doctor. "I know you must love Lucie very much to put your own wishes last."

"Doctor Manette, like you I left France of my own will. Pushed away by the suffering there, I look to a fresh start in England. I want to tie Lucie close to both of us, not take her away from you."

"And has Lucie told you that she loves you?"

"No, and I have not come to ask that. I came to tell you my feelings, nothing more. If Lucie ever tells you that she loves me, I hope it will make you happy."

"If she ever tells me so, I will give her to you," answered the doctor.

"I could not hope to wed Lucie if I had any secrets from you. There is something that I want you to know. I changed my name after I came to England...."

"Stop!" cried the doctor, covering his ears with his hands. The doctor's face turned white. "Don't tell me now. I don't want to hear it! If Lucie should love you, tell me on your wedding day, not before. Now, it is late and I don't think Lucie should see us together. Go now. And God be with you."

It was dark when Darnay left the doctor. Some time later, Lucie came home. "Father!" she called. But the doctor did not answer.

Then she heard the quiet tapping of a hammer in his room.

Charles Darnay was not the only man in London who loved Lucie Manette. At night, Sydney Carton often found himself standing in front of the Manette's home. He would stand there until the morning sun pushed him away.

Sydney Carton kept his feelings inside. He never told anyone that he loved Lucie, because he knew they would laugh at him. He had no hope that Lucie would ever love him. But he did want her to know that he cared.

A few days after Darnay talked with the doctor, Carton took it upon himself to visit Lucie. He found her at home alone.

"Mr. Carton!" she said as she answered the door. "You do not look well. Do come in and sit down."

"No, I am not well," he answered, stepping into the living room. His eyes were red and puffed up. His skin was a sick-looking gray. "Wine does not make one well."

"Then why not change, Mr. Carton?" she asked in a quiet voice. She looked at him with her soft face. She was surprised to see tears in his eyes.

"It is too late for me to change," he answered. "Every day I drink more wine. I will never be any better than I am." Sydney Carton covered his eyes with his hand. "Please forgive me," he went on. "I break down because of what I want to tell you. May I go on?"

"If it will make you happy, I will listen to you," Lucie answered.

"Sitting before you is a man who loves you, Miss Manette. But I know you could never love me, and I am glad. If you loved me, I would only fill your days with suffering."

"Even without loving you, can't I help you, Mr. Carton?" said Lucie. "Your heart is filled with love. Can't we use that love to build you into the man you want to be?"

"No, Miss Manette," Carton answered. "I can't change, and I can't hope to win your love. It is too late for that. But I will always be happy knowing that you listened to me. You cared enough to keep my words close to your heart. I will never hurt you by telling anyone about our talk today."

"And I will keep your secret, too, Mr. Carton."

"Thank you, Miss Manette." Sydney Carton seemed to grow strong as he talked. "Know that no matter how cold I may seem, I will always love you. I will do anything to keep you happy. The time will come when you will wed and have little children running around you. I want you to know this—*I would go to my death to keep your loved ones near you!*"

Sydney Carton took Lucie's hand and kissed it. "I must go now," he finished. "God be with you, Miss Manette."

6 Knitting

Madame Defarge was sitting in the dark room above the wine shop. She knitted as she listened to five men tell about Gaspard.

Monsieur Defarge began. "Jacques One! Jacques Two! Jacques Three! This man in the blue cap witnessed everything. Tell us what you saw, Jacques Five."

"I first saw Gaspard the evening before the Marquis was killed." The man in the blue cap went on. "He was running along the road, near the Marquis' chateau."

"And did you see him again after the killing?" asked Monsieur Defarge.

"Not for almost a year," answered Jacques Five. "I heard that he was hiding and that guards were looking for him. I did not see him again until last week."

"Where did you see him?" asked Jacques One.

"I was working on the road. The sun was about to set, and I was getting ready to go home. I looked up the road and saw six guards. Gaspard was with them. His arms were tied to his sides. The men walked close to me, and I followed them into town."

"How did they care for the prisoner?" asked Jacques Two.

"I watched the guards push him with their guns. They pushed him until he fell. Then they laughed at him. When they got through town, they put him in the Bastille."

"How long was he there?" asked Jacques Three.

"Until Sunday night," answered the man with the blue cap. "On Sunday night, the guards went to the Bastille to get him. They marched Gaspard through the town and stopped near the town well. There the guards set up the gallows. And on top of the gallows, they placed a knife, pointed up. They hanged Gaspard there. And his blood colored our drinking water!"

"How long did he hang over the well?" asked Monsieur Defarge.

"He is still hanging there," answered Jacques Five.

"Thank you for telling us the story," said Monsieur Defarge. "Please wait for me outside. I want to talk with these men alone."

"And what do you say, Jacques?" Jacques One asked. "To be listed?"

"To be listed for death!" answered Monsieur Defarge.

"The chateau and all the family?" asked Jacques One.

"*All* the family!" answered Defarge. "Every Evremonde shall be killed!"

"Is our list secret?" asked Jacques Two. "Are you sure no one else will find it?"

"Quite secret!" answered Defarge. "No one but Madame Defarge can read it. She has knitted the words with her own hands. The signs she uses are her secret. No one else will even guess what she is knitting."

"Fine!" answered Jacques Two. "It is good. All the family shall be killed!"

The men left the little room, one by one. At last, the Defarges went back to their wine shop.

"The policeman, Jacques Ten, stopped me on the street," Defarge said to his wife.

"And what did your friend tell you?"

"He said that we should watch for new spies around here. He knows of one man already—an Englishman."

"And does he know the man's name?" asked Madame Defarge.

"John Barsad," answered Defarge.

"What does he look like?"

"He is about 40 years old, five feet ten, with black hair. His face is long and thin. And his nose turns down at the end."

"I will list him in the morning."

The woman counted the money they made from selling wine that day. Monsieur Defarge shut the windows and closed the shop for the night.

The following morning, Madame Defarge sat at a table near the wine shop door, knitting. Beside her on the table was a small red flower. A few men were sitting or standing in the room. Some were drinking. Others were just talking.

Out of the corner of her eye, Madame Defarge saw a man come into the shop. She had never seen him before. He was about 40 years old, five feet ten, with black hair. Madame Defarge knew who—and what—the man was.

Without looking at the spy, Madame Defarge took the red flower in her hand. As she put the flower in her hair, the men in the shop stopped talking. One by one, they went out the door.

"Good day," said the Englishman.

"Good day," answered Madame Defarge, knitting again.

"I would like some red wine," he said. Madame Defarge got up from her table and filled a cup with red wine. Then she picked up her knitting again.

"You knit very well," the spy went on.

"I am glad you think so," she replied. *J-O-H-N*, she thought. *Stay here long enough and I will knit BARSAD, too.*

"You are new here, are you not?" asked Madame Defarge. "I would like you to meet Monsieur Defarge." Defarge was coming into the wine shop just then.

"I am happy to meet you," Barsad said to Monsieur Defarge. "You have a nice shop here. I heard of it when I was in England. I believe Doctor Manette stayed here after he left the Bastille."

"That is right," said Monsieur Defarge.

"His child came here to find her father. She took him back to England," said the spy.

"Yes, and that is the last we heard of them," said Monsieur Defarge.

"You might like to know that they are doing very well in London," Barsad went on. "Miss Manette is going to be wed. You may know the man. He is the nephew of Monsieur the Marquis. But in England he does not use his family name, Evremonde. In London he is called Charles Darnay."

Madame Defarge did not take her eyes off her knitting. Her hands moved very fast. She said nothing. Monsieur Defarge tried to fill a cup with wine, but his hands were shaking.

John Barsad looked at Defarge's hands and then placed money on the table. "Thank you for the wine," he said. Then he walked out of the shop.

"Can it be?" Defarge asked his wife.

"It can."

"If it is, I hope that Charles Darnay never comes to France. He is listed with all his family—his wife and children, too."

"He is listed with all his family," Madame Defarge echoed. Her face was hard and her voice was cold. She sat there knitting until night fell around her.

7 A Wedding

"It is such a beautiful day for your wedding," Doctor Manette said to Lucie. "The sky is blue, and the sun is shining down on you."

"Oh, Father, I am so happy," said Lucie. "We both love you so very much! That is why we are making our home with you. The three of us will always be together!"

Doctor Manette kissed Lucie. "It is almost time to go to the church," he said. "Get ready. I will be with you soon. But first there is something I must do."

Charles Darnay was waiting for the doctor in another room. When the two men were alone together, Doctor Manette closed the door. "Doctor," Darnay said. "You once asked me to wait until my wedding day to talk with you. It is time to tell you about my family and why I came to England."

"And I am ready to listen," answered the doctor in a quiet voice.

"I left France because I could not stand to watch the suffering of the people. My family was part of the nobility. My mother was kind and wanted to help the poor. But my father and my uncle did not care about the people. They looked upon the poor as if they were dogs. I tried to change them, but I could not. That is why I left France."

"Is your family still living?" asked the doctor, his face turning white at Darnay's words.

"No. I lost my father and mother when I was a child. My uncle was killed last year."

The doctor seemed to be afraid of something. "And your family name? What was your family name?" asked the doctor.

"Evremonde."

All at once, the doctor's hands began shaking. "I have heard enough! Let's go to the church!"

Mr. Lorry was waiting in the front hall with Lucie. "The coach is here," he said. "It is such a pretty day for a wedding. Oh, Lucie, how beautiful you are!"

"Are you ready to go to church, child?" asked Doctor Manette, coming into the hall.

"Yes, Father," she answered. Lucie looked at Charles Darnay with loving eyes. She did not see her father's white face.

The wedding was small and beautiful. When it was over, Lucie and Charles left for their honeymoon. "We will be back in a week," Lucie said. "We love you very much."

Doctor Manette kissed Lucie good-by. Turning to Darnay he said, "Take her, Charles. She is now your wife."

"And I will care for her with all my heart," Darnay answered. They waved good-by as the coach pulled away from the church. The others watched until the coach was far down the road.

Mr. Lorry took Doctor Manette home. When they were alone in the Manettes' living room, Mr. Lorry looked at the doctor. *He has that old lost look again*, Mr. Lorry thought. *He seems so afraid, so changed.*

The doctor sat alone and said nothing. His thoughts were far away and secret. He sat still for a long time. Then he got up from his chair. Without a word, the doctor went to his room and closed the door.

Soon Mr. Lorry heard a tapping sound. "My God!" said Mr. Lorry. "He is making shoes again!"

Mr. Lorry opened the door to the old man's room. He went in and stood beside the doctor. "Doctor Manette, what are you doing?"

"I am making a lady's walking shoe," he answered in a quiet voice. "I should have finished it before. I must finish it now." The old man kept tapping at the shoe. His voice and eyes seemed to be far away.

"Do you know me?" asked Mr. Lorry. "Do you know who I am?"

The doctor did not answer. He just kept tapping, tapping at the shoe. The doctor worked on the shoe for six days. All that time, he never said a word.

Mr. Lorry took time off from Tellson's Bank to watch over his friend. He was afraid that Lucie's wedding had been a death-blow to the old man. He was afraid the doctor would never be himself again.

At last, day seven came. Lucie and Charles would be home that evening. Mr. Lorry knew he would have to tell them about the doctor.

Mr. Lorry woke up that morning, afraid of what the day would bring. He went to the doctor's room and opened the door. To his surprise, Mr. Lorry found the doctor sitting near the window, reading. The hammer and nails had been put away.

The doctor looked up from his book as if nothing had happened. "Oh, Mr. Lorry," he said. "Good morning. It is such a beautiful day!"

Lucie and Charles came home late that afternoon. The doctor looked well and rested. Mr. Lorry did not tell them what happened while they were gone.

The family was happy to be together again. They had been together a short while when they heard a knock at the door. It was Sydney Carton.

"I came to give you my best wishes," he said to the Darnays. Then, turning to Charles Darnay, he said, "I hope we may be friends."

"We are already friends, I hope," Darney answered.

Sydney Carton was to become a good friend. He visited the family many times in the next seven years. In time, the Darnays had a baby girl. They named her Lucie. Little Lucie had yellow hair, like her mother. The child was always happy to see Carton.

The sound of laughter filled the hearts of this small family. But other sounds came into their home as well. For many years they heard far-away sounds of a storm building up in France. These were quiet sounds until little Lucie turned six years old. Then, near her birthday, the sounds grew loud. A great storm echoed across the sea.

8 The Bastille—1789

"The great storm begins!" cried out Defarge. "Today we will be glad to give up our lives! People of France, take up your guns!"

Outside the wine shop, the street was filled with people. A loud roar of voices covered up the sound of banging guns. There was no look of suffering on these faces now—only hate.

"Stay near me, Jacques Three!" cried Defarge. "Jacques One and Two, go to the head of the people. My wife, where will you be today?"

"I will be with you now," Madame Defarge answered. "But later I will be with the women!" She held an ax in her right hand. In her pocket she carried a small gun and a knife.

"Come then!" cried Defarge. "Friends, we are ready! On to the Bastille!"

The voices of 20,000 people cried out the hated word "Bastille!" The living sea of faces moved on through the streets. Wave upon wave, they hurried from the city.

With cannons, guns, and rocks, the people stormed the Bastille. Fire and smoke were all around them. Some fell to the ground, hurt. Others went to their death, smiling. And the sea of faces pushed on. At last, the drawbridge gave way. The feet of 20,000 poor people hurried across it, into the Bastille.

"Women, follow me!" cried Madame Defarge. "We can kill as well as the men." Ax in hand, Madame Defarge hurried across the drawbridge.

Other cries were heard. "The prisoners! Let them out!"

"The papers! Throw them in the fire!"

"The secret rooms! Find them!"

Killing guards as they went, the people stormed through the Bastille. They opened all the cages and let the prisoners out. They looked into every dark corner of the Bastille.

Defarge took hold of a guard. With his knife at the man's neck, Defarge said, "Take me to the North Tower! Quick!"

Defarge and Jacques Three followed the guard. They walked through dark, wet halls and into rooms where there was never any sun. They climbed down some steps. At last, they were alone and far away from the loud noise in the Bastille.

"This is the North Tower," the guard said with a shaking voice.

"Take us to 105 North Tower," Defarge told him.

"But there is no one there," the guard answered.

"Take us there!" cried Defarge, pushing the knife into the man's skin.

"Come this way." The guard took the two men up some dark steps. He pointed to a door. "This is the room you want." He opened the door, and the three men went in.

The room was small. There was one little window covered with heavy bars. And there was a chair, a table, and a bed. At the far end of the room, they saw a chimney. It too, was covered with bars.

"Hold the light near these walls," Defarge said to the guard. "I want to look at them."

The guard did as he was told. Then Defarge cried out, "Stop! Look at this!"

"'A. M.'" cried Jacques Three. "Alexandre Manette! This was his room then."

"Look around for a note or something," said Defarge, cutting into the bed with his knife. He then used his ax to break the table and chair to pieces. But he found nothing.

Then Defarge went over to the chimney. He put his hands through the bars and felt the stones. Some sand fell to the floor as one of the stones moved. A minute later, Defarge put a piece of paper in his pocket. "I found what I was looking for. Let's go!"

They hurried back to the sea of people. The people were pointing at the head guard of the Bastille. Madame Defarge was standing next to him. "We must kill this man for the deaths of our friends today!" she cried out. People near her moved in on the head guard. One man cut at him with a knife. Others used axes. The head guard fell to the ground.

Madame Defarge stood over him with a cold-blooded look in her eyes. She put her foot on the man's neck. And with one blow, she cut off his head with her ax.

The sea of people, hungry for more blood, hurried out of the Bastille. Seven heads of seven guards were placed on sticks and carried through the streets.

There would be still more blood in the following weeks. The hate-filled faces of the poor were to be seen all over France. The nobility all over the country were pulled from their homes. Many heads were cut off. Men, women, and children were made prisoners in the Bastille. Many chateaus went up in fire.

So ended the Evremonde chateau. The fire filled the night sky with red light. Near the chateau, the fire threw its dancing light on the home of Monsieur Gabelle. Charles Evremonde had asked Gabelle to care for the family house. He had told Gabelle to let the poor people use it.

Monsieur Gabelle watched the smoke and fire from his window. And then he saw the hate-filled faces coming after him. He closed his door with heavy bars and waited.

9 Pulled to France – 1792

For three more years, the storm of blood and death moved over France. For three more years, people in England listened to the hated sounds.

Because Tellson's Bank had branches in both Paris and London, it heard these sounds first. French nobility who had seen the storm coming moved their money from Paris to London. Those who came into England from France went to Tellson's first. Because of this, Tellson's became the place to find old friends.

One hot August afternoon, Charles Darnay was visiting Mr. Lorry at Tellson's Bank. They were sitting at Mr. Lorry's desk, talking in quiet voices.

"So you think I am too old?" asked Mr. Lorry, smiling.

"I think Paris is a bad place for you to go," answered Darnay.

"No one will hurt a man who is 78 years old," answered Mr. Lorry. "I must go, Charles. I am the only man at Tellson's who knows Paris well. There is work to be done there, and I must do it. Many people will be killed if Tellson's papers are found. I must go through the papers and set fire to some of them."

"I wish I were going," said Darnay, thinking out loud.

"What! You are a Frenchman! You know what might happen to you if you went there. The people are like animals, made wild by all the killing and the blood. It is good that you are far away."

"Mr. Lorry, it is because I am a Frenchman that I should go. I love my country and its people. They might listen to me. Blood might be saved."

"Or your blood might be lost," warned Mr. Lorry. "It is best that you stay here with Lucie."

"And when do you go to Paris?"

"I will go later today."

As they were talking, a letter was placed in front of Mr. Lorry. "Have you found the man whose name is on this letter?" another man from Tellson's asked.

"No," answered Mr. Lorry. "The letter is to go to the Marquis St. Evremonde of France. No one here has ever heard of him."

"He was the nephew of the late Marquis, I believe," said the man. "He hid from the people and left France after his uncle was killed. I am glad I never knew him. The people will kill him now for sure."

Darnay could not hold himself back. He turned to Mr. Lorry and said, "I know Evremonde. I will take the letter to him."

With the letter in his pocket, Darnay left Tellson's. He made his way to a church, where he could be alone. There, he opened the letter and read it.

Prison of the Abbaye, Paris
June 21, 1792

Monsieur St. Evremonde,

I was taken prisoner from my home and marched along the road to Paris. After much suffering, I know I will soon be put to death.

They say I am a prisoner because I kept the chateau for you. I told them that I worked to better their lives, but they don't believe me. I took no taxes from the people. I did as you asked.

Their only answer to me is, "Where is Evremonde?" I can be saved if they can talk with you.

I hope this letter gets to you and that you can help me. I was a good friend to you. I ask that you be a good friend to me —before it is too late.

Your servant,
Gabelle

Charles Darnay sat in the quiet of the church, thinking. He knew the suffering that his family had brought on the poor people. But he himself had never hurt anyone. *I am sure the people will listen to me. And I must help Gabelle*, he thought. *I will go to France tomorrow night.*

That evening, Darnay sat down to write a letter to Lucie and her father. He told why he had to go to France. And he said that he would come back soon. He placed the letter where Lucie would find it the following night.

The next day went by. Darnay did not tell Lucie or the doctor his plans. When evening came, Darnay kissed his wife and child. "I have a meeting to go to, my love. I will be home in a little while," he said.

Then, with a heavy heart, Charles Darnay left for Dover on his way to France.

10 The Prisoner

Riding to Paris was slow in the fall of 1792. Every town had a band of people at the city gate. With guns at the ready, the bands watched every new face. The guards looked at the papers men carried with them. And they looked on secret lists for the travellers' names.

Charles Darnay did not get very far his first night in France. He found himself a room while he was still a long way from Paris. He went to bed very tired.

But he did not sleep very long. A loud banging on the door woke him up. Two men came into his room and sat on his bed. They were wearing red caps and carried guns.

"Run-away," said one of the men. "We are going to take you to Paris—under guard."

"I would like nothing better than to get to Paris," answered Darnay. "But I don't need the guard."

"Shut up, nobility!" cried one of the red-caps. He hit Darnay with his gun. "Get up and get dressed!"

Darnay did as he was told. Soon, the three men were on horses, riding to Paris. They rode until the sun came up. They waited off the road during the day. When night came, they moved on again. At last, morning found them at the city gate outside Paris.

"Where are this prisoner's papers?" asked the guard at the gate.

"I am not a prisoner!" Darnay said. "You can see that I came to France of my own will."

"Where are the prisoner's papers?" the guard asked again.

The red-cap handed Gabelle's letter to the guard. "Monsieur Defarge, this man comes back from England. There he is called Darnay. We know him as Evremonde."

Defarge read the letter and then gave Darnay a careful look. "Open the gate!" he said at last. Defarge took Darnay into the guard-room. On the desk was a list of names. "How old are you, Evremonde?" he asked.

"I am 37."

"Where is your wife?"

"In England."

"That is good. You will be sent to Prison of La Force."

"What for?" asked Darnay. "I have done nothing."

"You, a run-away, have come back to France. That breaks our laws. Now follow me." Defarge walked Darnay through the streets of Paris. "You may know my name," Defarge went on. "I keep a wine shop. I was a friend of Doctor Manette."

"Will you help me then?" Darnay asked. "I must let my family know what has happened."

"No," answered Defarge. "I work for my country and my people. I will do nothing for you."

At last, the men came to Prison of La Force. A fat man opened the heavy door. Defarge presented the prisoner, "Monsieur St. Evremonde!" He handed the fat man some papers and walked away.

The fat man looked at the papers. " *'In secret'*," he read. "Come, follow me." They walked together through the dark, wet halls. After climbing some steps, they came at last to a room. The guard opened the lock and took Darnay into the room.

Darnay looked around him. He was surprised to see women prisoners sitting around a long table. Some were knitting. Others were reading or writing. Men prisoners stood beside their wives. And children sat on the floor.

As Darnay came into the room, the prisoners stood up to meet him. One man walked up to Darnay and said, "Our home is your home. May your stay be short and its ending happy. May I ask your name?"

"I am Charles Darnay Evremonde, nephew of the late Marquis."

"I hope you are not to be kept in secret," the man went on.

"I heard them say I was," Darnay answered.

"We hope it will not be for long. Some of our friends were in secret for a short time only."

The guard pushed Darnay to a door on the other side of the room. They went through the door and up 40 steps. At the top of the steps, there was a small door. It opened into a small, cold room.

"This is your room," said the guard.

"Why am I to be locked up alone?"

"I don't know," answered the guard. The fat man closed the door and went away.

The prisoner stood in his room, listening as the sounds of the city came through his window. He walked across the small floor over and over again. *I am left here alone*, he thought. *No one knows where I am.*

Then his thoughts turned to Doctor Manette. *He made shoes. He made shoes. He made shoes.*

11 Waiting

Tellson's Bank let a large house in Paris for Mr. Lorry to work in. The 78-year-old man worked late into the night each evening. He had been in Paris for almost a week. Already, he was afraid of what was happening around him.

Sitting alone in this house, Mr. Lorry thought about the things he saw. *Thank God I have no friends in Paris now. May God save all the prisoners and their families who are near death!* Just then, the bell at the city gate sounded. *They are back!* he thought. He listened for other sounds.

All at once, the door near him opened. A man and a woman hurried into the room. "Lucie! Doctor Manette!" Mr. Lorry called out, surprised. "What are you doing here? What is the matter?"

"Charles is here in Paris," answered Lucie.

"He has been here for three or four days," the doctor went on. "They stopped him at the gate and sent him to La Force. He is a prisoner!" The doctor let out a cry.

The bell at the city gate sounded again. Heavy feet and loud voices moved into the streets. The doctor ran to the window. "What was that?" he asked.

"Don't look out!" cried Mr. Lorry. "Don't watch them!"

The doctor turned to Mr. Lorry with a grave smile. "My friend," he said. "I was once a Bastille prisoner in this city. Knowing that, these people would never hurt me. Knowing that, they would let me go places others could not go. They will give me news of Charles. Because of it, I know I can help Charles."

The doctor turned to the window again. "What was that noise?" he asked, looking out to the street.

There he saw 40 or 50 people standing near a round stone. Two men turned the stone on a wheel, while others sharpened axes on it. Every hand, face, and ax was covered with fresh blood.

The doctor turned to Mr. Lorry with a look of wonder in his eyes. "They are killing the prisoners," Mr. Lorry said in a soft voice. "If you think it will help Charles, go tell them who you are. Already it may be too late!"

The doctor hurried from the room and ran into the street. Mr. Lorry watched from the window. The old man went to the sharpening stone. The hate-filled people looked at the doctor and listened. The sharpening stone stopped turning for a minute. All at once, the people took the doctor by the arm. They cried out, "Long live the Bastille prisoner! Help the Bastille prisoner's family in La Force! Save the prisoner Evremonde!" The blood-covered people carried the doctor off to La Force.

Three more times that night the bell sounded at the gate. And three more times the sharpening stone made its death-filled noise. But Doctor Manette did not come back.

The night ended and morning came. Morning gave way to afternoon, and afternoon to night. There was still no doctor. At last, Mr. Lorry heard a banging at the door.

A man stood outside the door with a letter in his hand. A woman stood beside him, knitting. "Mr. Lorry?" the man said. "I have come with a letter from Doctor Manette. My name is Defarge. This is my wife. We met you once at my wine shop."

"Yes. What news do you bring?" asked Mr. Lorry.

Defarge handed Mr. Lorry the letter. Mr. Lorry read it out loud: " 'Charles still lives. I must stay at La Force for a while to help him. Defarge is a friend. Let him see Lucie'."

Mr. Lorry brought Monsieur Defarge and his wife into the house. "Is Madame Defarge to see Lucie, too?"

"Yes, she must see the girl and know her face. My wife will watch out for her. She will see that nothing bad happens to her."

Mr. Lorry called to Lucie. Lucie came into the room with her little girl. "I believe you know Monsieur and Madame Defarge," said Mr. Lorry. "They came to tell us that Charles and your father are well. They came to see you, too. You and little Lucie will be under their care."

"Thank you for helping us," Lucie said with a warm voice. "You bring such happy news." She took Madame Defarge's hand and kissed it.

Madame Defarge pulled her hand away and dropped it to her side. She gave Lucie and the child a cold look. "We have seen them well enough," the woman said. "Let us go!" The Defarges turned to the door.

"Please be good to Charles!" asked Lucie. "Please do what you can for him."

"We will do nothing for him," said Madame Defarge. "It is you and the child we will look after. All our lives we have seen our families suffer. My people have stood this suffering for a long time. Do you think we care about your suffering now?" The cold-blooded woman went out the door.

Doctor Manette did not come back to Mr. Lorry's for four days. When he did, he told them the grave news of what had happened while he was gone. "In these four days, 1,100 prisoners were killed. At La Force, I witnessed the hearings. Each prisoner sat alone before five judges. One after another, they were sent out to be killed. A few were let go. Some were sent back to their rooms. Charles is still a prisoner, but he has been saved."

"When will we have him back?" asked Lucie.

"I don't know," answered her father. "But I asked if I could work at La Force. I will care for sick prisoners and guards. That way, I will see Charles often. We will be sure he is all right."

Doctor Manette saw Darnay every week. But he never could get the people to let Darnay go. The wave of hate was moving across France too fast for that. More than 300,000 men were working to tear down the old government. The King was tried, and his head was cut off. Marie Antoinette, too, lost her head to the new Queen of France—La Guillotine.

Doctor Manette knew that he was the only man who could help Charles. This made him strong. He was strong, too, because he could help the other prisoners in their suffering.

For more than a year, the doctor worked in La Force. For more than a year, Lucie waited. Every day she walked near La Force, hoping Charles might see her from his window.

At last, one December day, Lucie stood near La Force. Doctor Manette came out to meet her and give her news. "You will see Charles soon," he said. "He will be tried tomorrow! We must tell Mr. Lorry!"

12 Judged

Before Charles Darnay was called into the court-room, 15 other prisoners were tried. All 15 were going to be put to death the following day.

At last, Darnay was called. "Charles Evremonde, called Darnay!" Darnay followed a guard into the courtroom. He looked around the room and saw Lucie. Doctor Manette and Mr. Lorry were with her. Then he turned and saw Monsieur Defarge. Madame Defarge was next to him, knitting.

"You are being tried as a run-away," one of the judges said. "You came back to this country from England. That breaks our laws!"

"Off with his head!" cried the people. "To La Guillotine! *Off with his head!*"

"But I came back as a friend to France," Darnay answered. "I gave up my name and my home here. I wanted to live by my own work, not by the work of the poor people around me. My home was to be used for the people."

"Can you prove what you say?" asked another judge.

"Yes. I have two witnesses, my friends Gabelle and Alexandre Manette."

"But you took an English woman as your wife," the first judge said.

"Yes, but she came from France. Her father is the good doctor that you all know well, Doctor Manette."

All at once, the cold faces in the room became warm. Happy cries were heard across the courtroom. "Our friend the doctor!" some called out. "Let us hear from him."

Doctor Manette took the stand. "Charles Darnay is a good man," he said, "and he loves France. He was one of my first friends when I got out of the Bastille. He wed my only child and has been good to both of us." The people looked at Darnay with smiling faces. "Charles is a friend to France. He was tried in England as a spy—because of his love for this country. He was almost put to death!"

A cry went out from the people. "Our friend, Charles Darnay Evremonde! Why did he come back to France?"

The doctor answered their cries. "Charles came back to save his friend, Gabelle. Gabelle was to be put to death because he watched over Evremonde's chateau. Should Charles be killed because he loved his friend—and his country?"

"No!" cried the people. "Let him go! Save the good man, Evremonde!"

"We have heard enough," said the first judge. "The jury is ready."

One at a time the five judges said, "Not guilty!" Each time it was said, the people let out a happy cry.

When it was over, the people hurried up to Charles Darnay to shake his hand. With tears in their eyes, they all wished him well. As the family left the courtroom, Doctor Manette looked for Monsieur Defarge. He wanted to thank him. But both the Defarges were gone.

The happy family went back to Mr. Lorry's Paris home. More than a year of suffering was over now. But the feeling of death still fell around them.

Little Lucie was happy to see her father again. "Can we go home now?" she asked.

"No, we must wait a little while," answered Darnay. "But we will go home as soon as we can."

The family sat in the living room. They talked about the happy times they would have together again. Little Lucie fell asleep in her father's arms.

Their hearts were quiet at last. But all at once, Lucie jumped up. "What was that?" she cried. "I heard feet on the steps outside!"

Doctor Manette listened for a minute. Then he turned to Lucie. "There is no one on the steps," he said. "They are as quiet as death."

But as the doctor said the last word, there was a knock at the door. "Father! We must hide Charles!" cried Lucie.

"There is no need for that, my child. Charles has already been tried and found not guilty. No one is after him now. Let me see who is at the door." The doctor crossed the room and opened the door.

Four strong men, armed with guns, came into the room. "Evremonde!" called the first man.

"Who wants him?" Darnay answered.

"We all want him. You are Evremonde. We saw you today. You are again a prisoner of France!" The four men stepped up to Darnay. Lucie and the child were holding him.

"What have I done? I was found not guilty this afternoon."

"You will know tomorrow. You will be tried tomorrow."

The doctor turned to the men. "Do you know me?" he asked.

"Yes, we know you, Doctor Manette."

"Will you then tell me what has happened?"

"We can tell you only that Evremonde has been denounced."

"Who denounced him?"

"Two men denounced him. One man is Monsieur Defarge. We can't tell you the other man's name. Tomorrow you will know."

13 A Spy is Seen

Only Mr. Lorry knew that Charles Darnay had a secret friend in France. The day before the hearing, Sydney Carton came to Paris. He knew that a jury might find Darnay guilty. Carton went to Mr. Lorry at Tellson's Bank. But he did not want Lucie to know he was in town.

Carton stood outside La Force when the first hearing was going on. He watched people come and go as he waited for news about Darnay. While he stood there, Carton saw a man he once knew. He followed the man from La Force into Defarge's wine shop. He listened as the man talked with one of his friends. Then Carton followed him outside.

"I know you from London," Carton said to the man. "You are English. Why do you wear the Frenchman's red cap?"

"You must be thinking of another man," the man said, pushing Carton away. "Go away. Leave me alone!"

"No, you are John Barsad. You were a witness when my friend was tried in London. Please come with me to Tellson's Bank."

"Why should I?" said Barsad.

"Because we are going to meet Mr. Lorry there when today's hearing is over. You may be of some help to Charles!"

"And if I don't want to help?" asked the spy.

"Then I think the French people might like to know what I know about you," Carton answered. "Why have you changed your name?"

"Wait! Wait! Enough. I will go," Barsad answered.

In a few minutes, the two men were sitting with Mr. Lorry. "Charles is a prisoner again," said Carton. "I heard Barsad tell his friend over a cup of wine."

"Can Doctor Manette save him this time?" asked Mr. Lorry, surprised and afraid.

"I hope so, but I am not sure," said Carton. "He could not stop them from taking him away. This is a changing game, Mr. Lorry. The people may carry a man home today and kill him tomorrow. Let Doctor Manette play the winning game. I have found us a friend in La Force." Carton gave Barsad a careful look.

"And what makes you think your new-found friend will help?" asked Barsad. His face was cold and hard.

"I think you will help," answered Sydney Carton. "I know too much about you. First you were a guard, then a prisoner, and now a guard again.

You have changed your name, and the French do not know you are Barsad."

Carton looked down at Barsad's hand. It was shaking. The spy knew his old name was knitted in Madame Defarge's list. He knew he would be killed if Carton told about this.

"Shall I go on?" Carton asked. "You once worked for the English government. Now you work for the new French government. But you are still getting your pay from England! If you do not help us, Mr. Barsad, I will denounce you to the French!"

"I can't do much. What is it you want?" asked Barsad.

"I ask you to do very little. You are a guard at La Force. Am I right?"

"Yes, but I can't let Evremonde go!"

"I ask only this," Carton said. "If Charles is found guilty tomorrow, you will let me visit him at once."

"And you will not say anything about who I am?" asked Barsad.

"I will stay quiet about it."

"Then I will let you visit the prisoner," answered Barsad. "Now, I must go to work." The spy got up from his chair and left Tellson's Bank.

When Barsad had gone, Mr. Lorry turned to Sydney Carton. "If Charles is found guilty, your visit will not stop his death."

"I never said it would," answered Carton.

A look of suffering crossed the old man's face.

"You are a good friend," Carton went on. "You are loved by so many. You have done many good things for people. They will miss you when you are gone. I have done nothing good all my life." Carton was quiet for a minute. Then he turned and walked to the door. "It is time for me to go. Good night, Mr. Lorry."

It was late at night when Sydney Carton left Tellson's Bank. He walked to La Force. Standing outside, he looked at its small windows and heavy gates. A while later, Carton walked into town and went into a drug store. He picked up two small bags and handed them to the druggist.

"Be careful of those drugs," the druggist said to Carton. "Don't put them together."

Carton gave the man money and thanked him. He placed the bags in his pocket. Then he walked out of the store. *There is nothing else to do*, he thought. *Tomorrow I can help.*

Sydney Carton could not sleep that night. He walked around the city until morning. For the first time, Carton looked strong. He held his head high and thought about God.

When morning came, he washed up and went to the courtroom.

14 Judged Again

There were many people in the courtroom that morning. Sydney Carton was pushed into a far corner of the room. He could see Lucie sitting beside her father.

Before long, Charles Darnay was brought before the jury. Lucie gave him a loving look, and Darnay seemed to grow strong. Had anyone looked at Sydney Carton, he would have seen love and hope in his face, too.

But every face was watching the jury. The five judges looked like starving dogs getting ready to tear a deer to pieces. The first judge began, "Evremonde, called Darnay, you have been denounced."

"By what man?" Darnay asked.

"By three people—Monsieur Defarge, his wife, and Doctor Alexandre Manette!"

A great roar came from the people. All eyes turned to the doctor. He was now standing where he had been sitting a minute before. His face was white and his hands were shaking.

"*No!* That is a lie!" the doctor cried out. "I have not denounced him! You know that he is part of my family. I have worked to save this man. Who is it who lies and says I denounced him?"

"Be quiet!" said the judge. "France matters more than your family. You must be willing to give up even your own child if France asks you to. Listen to what follows—and be quiet!"

Doctor Manette sat down, shaking. He pulled Lucie close to him and listened.

"Monsieur Defarge," the first judge said. "You may begin."

Defarge took the stand. "I was once a servant of Doctor Manette," he said. "And I was his friend. As you know, he was a prisoner in the Bastille for almost 18 years. When we took the Bastille in 1789, I went to 105 North Tower. There, behind a stone in the chimney, I found this paper." Defarge pulled a piece of paper from his pocket. Doctor Manette did not take his eyes off the paper.

Defarge began to read. " 'I, Alexandre Manette, write this letter from the Bastille. I will hide it in the chimney. People who live after me may find it here. It is December, 1767 and I have been a prisoner for 10 years. I am afraid that I do not have long to live.

" 'This is my story. In 1757, I was walking along the Seine River. A coach came near me and stopped. I was called over by the man in the coach, the Marquis St. Evremonde.

" 'The Marquis asked me to go with him. A woman was sick and needed doctoring. I went with the Marquis to his chateau. There I met the Marquis' brother. As I went into the house, I heard a woman crying out. The two brothers took me to her.

" 'The beautiful woman was about 20 years old. She was resting on a bed. Her arms were tied to her side. She did not know where she was. And she kept crying out, "My father! My brother!" She cried out these words over and over again.

"'Then Marquis St. Evremonde took me to another room. There I found a good-looking boy, about 17 years old. He lay on the floor. I saw at once he was near death. A knife had gone through his side.

"'I asked the boy what had happened. He pointed to the Marquis. "That man has robbed us of all we had," he said in a quiet voice. "He robbed us of land, of money, and of food. When there was nothing else to take, he tried to rob us of our sisters." The boy held his side. He was suffering very much.

"'The Marquis came to our home one day when I was in the fields. He had seen my sister and knew she was beautiful. He wanted her. But my sister was a good woman. She would not go with him. These men killed my father and took my sister away. The Marquis used her and kept her in this house.

"'When I came home, I found my father and learned what happened. I have another sister, who is still a child. I picked her up in my arms and carried her away. I hid her where the nobility would never find her. *She* would never be used by them." The boy's voice was very soft now.

" 'Then I came to the chateau. I tried to kill the Marquis, but he got me first." The boy tried to pick himself up, but he fell back into my arms.

" 'When morning came, the suffering of the brother and sister was over. They met their deaths as so many poor people do—at the hands of the nobility.' "

Defarge stopped reading for a minute. He gave Charles Evremonde a cold look. Then he read from the paper again.

" 'The Marquis tried to pay me, but I would not take his gold. I saw that he hated me, because I knew too much. A few days later, I was called out of my home. The Marquis picked me up in his coach and sent me here, to the Bastille. He and his brother said nothing to me. They said nothing to my wife. She now suffers as much as I.

" 'Because of this, I know they have no good in them. Because of this, I denounce them *and all their family*. I hope, some day, they will answer for what they have done.' "

A roar sounded in the courtroom. Defarge set the paper down. He took his seat beside Madame Defarge. The people roared again each time a judge said, "Guilty!" Five times they heard it. "Guilty!" "Guilty!" "Guilty!" "Guilty!" *"Guilty!"* Charles Darnay would be guillotined tomorrow.

15 Madame Defarge's Secret

Lucie felt sick at heart, but she knew she had to be strong for Charles. "Let me hold him once more," she asked the guard.

"Just once!" Barsad answered.

"Good-by, my love. We will be together soon," she said. "My heart will break, and I will meet you again in the next world."

"Kiss little Lucie for me," Darnay said to his wife.

Doctor Manette came up to him. "Forgive me! Forgive me!" he cried. Then tears filled his eyes.

"Don't feel that way, Doctor!" Darnay said, holding the old man. "I know now the suffering you went through when you first learned my name. I thank you for all the love you gave us. Take care of Lucie and the child for me."

Barsad pulled Darnay out of the courtroom. Lucie fell to the floor in tears. Then she blacked out. The doctor was not strong enough to pick her up. Sydney Carton moved out of the corner and took her in his arms. "Shall I take her to a coach?" he asked.

Carton carried her outside and placed her beside her father in a coach. He kissed Lucie's hand.

In a soft voice, he said, ". . . to keep your loved ones near you." And then he walked away.

I think it is best that I be seen, Carton thought. *The people should know that there is a man in Paris who looks like Charles.*

Carton walked across the city to the wine shop. He went in and sat down. Only Madame Defarge and Jacques Three were there.

Madame Defarge looked at Carton with surprise. She came up to him and asked, "English?"

"Yes, I am English," he answered.

Madame Defarge turned away. He heard her say, "He looks so much like Evremonde!" She brought Carton a cup of wine and went back to her table. A minute later, Defarge came into the shop. Carton listened to them talk in quiet voices.

"Are you happy?" Defarge asked his wife. "Evremonde will be killed tomorrow."

"Not happy enough," the woman answered. "I will be happy only when all the family is killed!"

"But the doctor has suffered so much. You have seen it on his face," Defarge said. "Would you make him suffer even more?"

"Would you save him?" she asked. "That family so hurt by the Marquis St. Evremonde was *my* family. That sister who was killed was *my* sister. That brother was *my* brother, and that father *my* father. For them I must see all the Evremonde family killed—*all!*"

A few people came into the wine shop, and Madame Defarge stopped talking. Carton put some money on the table and left.

After leaving the wine shop, Sydney Carton went straight to Mr. Lorry. "You must do as I say," he told him. "They plan to kill Lucie, the child, and even the doctor. Do you have papers that will let you get out of France?"

"Yes," answered Mr. Lorry. "We all do."

"Then this is what you must do. Early tomorrow afternoon, have your horses ready."

"I will."

"You and the family wait for me in the coach. When I come, take me in. As soon as my seat is filled, drive away. Will you do it?" asked Carton.

"Yes, I will do everything just as you say."

"You must not stop once my seat is filled. If you do, all the lives will be lost. Good-by, my friend."

"Good night, Mr. Carton," said Mr. Lorry.

Sydney Carton stepped out onto the street. He stood there for a little while. At last, he blew a kiss to Lucie's window. "God be with you," he said. And with that, he walked away.

16 La Guillotine

That night, 52 people waited for death. Charles Darnay waited alone in his room. He knew there was no hope for him. Darnay asked the guard for paper so that he could write letters to his friends. He finished a note to Lucie, telling her of his love. And he finished one to the doctor, placing Lucie in his care. Then he thought about Mr. Lorry and all he had done for the family. But Darnay never thought about Sydney Carton.

When the room became too dark to write, Darnay went to bed. But he could not sleep. *What does the guillotine look like?* he wondered. *I have never seen it. How high is it from the ground? How many steps will I have to walk up? Will the hands that kill me be red with blood? Which way will my face be turned? Will I see the knife coming down to cut off my head?* Charles Darnay was not afraid. He just wondered what death was going to be like.

Night ended and morning came. Darnay listened to the sounds of the city outside. He heard the bells ring the time. *I am to be guillotined at 3:00 this afternoon,* he thought. *I will be ready to go at 2:00.* As the morning went by, he listened to the bells. *Now 10:00 gone . . . . Now 11:00 gone . . . . Now*

12:00 gone. But when Darnay heard the bell ring 1:00, he also heard steps outside the door. *They are early*, he said to himself.

Darnay watched the door. It opened, and Sydney Carton stepped into the room. "Carton! I don't believe it is you!" Darnay said, surprised. "Are you a prisoner, too?"

"No, but I come from your wife," said Carton. "You must do as I say. Take off your shoes and put on the ones I am wearing. Quick!"

"Carton, we can't get out of here. You will only be killed with me."

"*We* will not get out. Now do as I say. Put on my hat and coat." Carton pushed Darnay's hands into the coat.

"Please, Carton, go away. We can't get out. No one ever has."

"Just do as I say. Sit down at your table and write what I tell you."

Darnay sat down to write and Carton stood beside him.

Carton placed his hand in his pocket. "Write this: *Secret words were said between us once. I have always kept them close to my heart*."

Carton pulled a small bag from his pocket. "Write on," he said. "*I am happy that I can prove them now*." As Darnay was writing, Carton moved the bag near the prisoner's nose.

Darnay's hand fell to the table. "What do I smell?" he asked. His eyes were starting to close. He was drugged.

"Go on writing," Carton answered.

But Darnay could not move his hand. His eyes closed, and he fell to the floor.

Carton finished changing clothes with the prisoner. Then he called to Barsad. "Come in! Quick! Help this man outside. Tell the guards he is sick. Get him to Mr. Lorry's before the drug wears off. Tell Mr. Lorry to drive away!"

Barsad left the room, holding Darnay up. The door closed, and Carton stood alone. He waited until he heard the bells ring 2:00. Then he listened as the guard came to his door.

"Follow me, Evremonde," the guard said. "Your time has come."

Carton followed the guard into a dark room at the end of the hall. Men, women, and girls were sitting there, waiting for death. The guard left the room, and a girl stepped up to Sydney. "Monsieur Evremonde," she said. "I met you when you first came to La Force." The girl was about 16 years old.

"Oh, yes," Carton said, afraid that the girl would see he was not Evremonde.

"Monsieur Evremonde, I am not afraid of dying." The girl looked at the floor. "But I don't see how my death will help the people. May I ride to the guillotine with you, Monsieur Evremonde? I have no family left, and you will help make me strong."

The girl looked up at his eyes. All at once, she knew. A look of surprise crossed her face, then wonder. "Are you dying for him?" she asked in a quiet voice.

"And his wife and child," Carton answered.

"What a good man you are! Will you let me hold your hand?"